SLIM & DELICIOUS
HIGH
FIBER
COOKBOOK

Marjorie Carter

Sweetwater Press
Florence, Alabama

Published by Sweetwater Press
P.O. Box 1855
Florence, Alabama 35631

Produced by The Triangle Group, Ltd.
227 Park Avenue
Hoboken, NJ 07030

Design: Tony Meisel
Special thanks to Risa Gary of Mikasa, New York
Origination and printing: Cronion S.A., Barcelona

Printed in Spain

ISBN 1-884822-07-X

Contents

Introduction

Fiber is a dietary necessity. It comes from fruits, vegetables and grains in varying degrees and is the best natural way to keep your digestive system going strong. Studies strongly indicate that a high-fiber diet can help prevent colon cancer, and it can certainly ease any minor digestive problems.

Too often, however, people think of high fiber as tasteless gruel or heavy "all natural" pastry. Nothing could be further from the truth! Foods high in fiber include apples, figs, pears, citrus (unstrained), peppers, carrots, potatoes, turnips, beans, peas, wheat, barley, brown rice and many, many others.

Pasta in all its variations is loaded with fiber, as are salads and greens. The fiber is most efficacious in uncooked forms, but is still mighty potent combined into a variety of tasty dishes, as evidenced herein. Remember, good crusty bread is a source as well.

Another advantage of many forms of high-fiber foods is that they are also excellent sources of complex carbohydrates, probably the largest chunk of one's nutritionally-sound daily diet.

As you will see from the recipes in this book, fiber can be both a benefit and a pleasure.

Note: Juicing has become very popular of late. The process removes the fiber from the fruits and vegetables. Consider this when planning your diet.

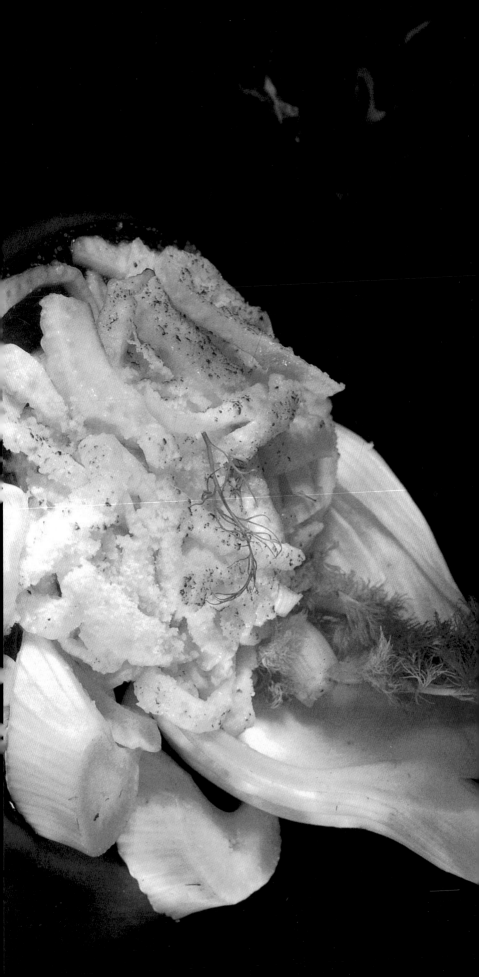

Baked Fennel with Parmesan Cheese

2 pounds fennel, tops trimmed and cut into thin slices
1 tablespoon lemon juice
3 tablespoons low-fat margarine
1 tablespoon olive oil
3/4 cup water
4 ounces freshly grated Parmesan cheese
freshly ground black pepper, to taste
salt, to taste

In a large bowl combine the fennel with the lemon juice. Toss and set aside for at least 15 minutes.

In a skillet melt 2 tablespoons of the margarine with the oil. Add the fennel (leaving behind the remaining juice) and sauté for 3 to 5 minutes or until transparent. Add the water to the skillet. Cover the skillet and cook over a medium-low heat for about 15 minutes or until tender. Drain the fennel in a colander or strainer.

Preheat the oven to 375 degrees F. Grease a 6-cup baking dish.

Season the fennel in the colander with the pepper and salt. Toss.

Layer the fennel in the baking dish and top each layer with grated cheese. Finish with grated cheese and top with the remaining tablespoon of margarine.

Bake for 20 to 25 minutes or until the fennel can be pierced easily with a fork and the top is brown. Serves 6.

Carrot-Pepper Sauté

2 tablespoons low-fat margarine
1 pound young carrots
1 red pepper
1 yellow pepper
2 tablespoons dry white wine
3 tablespoons water
1 tablespoon finely chopped fresh tarragon or
    1 teaspoon dried tarragon
freshly ground black pepper, to taste
salt, to taste

Peel and thinly slice the carrots.
    Top, core and rinse the peppers. Cut them into thin strips.
    In a large skillet melt the margarine. Add the carrots and cook for 3 to 5 minutes. Add the peppers, the wine and water. Cover and cook for 5 to 7 minutes or until all the vegetables are tender. Drain any remaining liquid.
    Toss with the tarragon, pepper and salt. Additional margarine may be added while you are tossing. Serves 6.

Red Cabbage & Apples

2 tablespoons low-fat margarine
1/4 pound slab bacon, cubed
1 medium head red cabbage, finely chopped
2 large Granny Smith apples, peeled, cored
   and thinly sliced
1/4 cup apple cider vinegar
2 tablespoons sugar, or to taste
freshly ground black pepper, to taste
salt, to taste

In a large skillet melt 2 tablespoons of margarine. Add the bacon and cook until it begins to brown. Add the cabbage, apples, vinegar, sugar, pepper and salt. Stir until well combined.
   Cover and cook until the cabbage is tender; about 35 to 40 minutes. Stir occasionally. Adjust seasoning to taste. Serves 8.

Rosemary Roasted Potatoes

4 pounds red or new potatoes
1/3 cup olive oil, or enough to coat
6 cloves of garlic, chopped
1/4 cup fresh rosemary, chopped
freshly ground black pepper, to taste
salt, to taste

Preheat the oven to 375 degrees F. Rinse the potatoes and cut into medium-size chunks.

In large bowl combine the potatoes, oil, garlic, rosemary and black pepper. Transfer the potatoes to a baking sheet large enough to hold them in a single layer.

Bake in the middle of the oven until golden brown and cooked through. This could take 45 to 60 minutes. Turn occasionally to ensure even roasting.

When done transfer to a serving bowl and season with salt and additional pepper if desired. Serves 6.

Brussels Sprouts with Hazelnuts

1/4 cup hazelnuts
6 tablespoons softened low-fat margarine
1 tablespoon finely chopped shallots
1 1/4 pounds fresh Brussels sprouts
freshly ground black pepper, to taste
salt, to taste

Preheat the oven to 350 degrees F. Place the hazelnuts in a shallow baking dish. Toast in the oven until lightly browned, 5 to 10 minutes. Remove the nuts from the oven and transfer to a clean kitchen towel. Rub the nuts in the towel to remove the skins.

Coarsely chop 8 of the hazelnuts. Set aside. Put the remaining nuts into a food processor or blender and process until finely ground.

Heat 1 tablespoon of the margarine in a skillet over a moderate heat. Add the shallots. Lower the heat and sauté until the shallots are soft, but not browned, about 5 minutes.

Remove the skillet from the heat and let the shallots cool to room temperature.

In a bowl combine the remaining margarine, ground hazelnuts and cooled shallots. Mix until well blended. Cover the bowl and refrigerate until needed.

Cook the Brussels sprouts in a large saucepan of lightly salted boiling water until tender, about 5 to 7 minutes. The cooking time will depend on the size of the sprouts. Drain well in a colander.

Remove the margarine-hazelnut mixture from the refrigerator. In a skillet, over a very low heat, melt the margarine. Break the margarine up with a spoon, do not let it get too hot or it will become oily. Add the Brussels sprouts to the skillet and toss until well-coated with the margarine mixture.

Transfer the sprouts to a serving bowl and sprinkle with the reserved nuts. Serves 4 to 6.

Broccoli & Roasted Red Pepper

1 large sweet red pepper
2 1/2 pounds fresh broccoli, trimmed into spears
3 garlic cloves, crushed
1/4 cup olive oil
1 small dried red chili pepper
salt, to taste

Put the red pepper onto a broiling pan and roast, turning frequently until blackened all over. Put the pepper into a paper bag and fold the bag closed. Let stand for 10 minutes, then remove from the bag. Peel and seed the pepper and cut it into 1/4 -inch strips. Set aside.

Cook the broccoli in a large pot of boiling water until just tender, about 5 to 7 minutes. Drain well again and gently pat dry. Set aside.

Heat the oil, garlic and chili pepper together in a skillet over high heat until bubbles form around the garlic. Lower the heat to moderately low and cook, stirring constantly until the garlic and chili pepper are light brown. Strain the mixture through a fine sieve into a bowl. Discard the remaining garlic and chili pepper in the sieve. Let the strained oil cook slightly and season with salt, if desired.

Generously brush the broccoli spears and roasted red pepper with the garlic oil. Transfer to a serving platter. Serves 6.

Sautéed Zucchini with Fresh Herbs

1 1/2 pounds zucchini, thinly sliced
4 tablespoons olive oil
2 tablespoons low-fat margarine
2 teaspoons finely chopped garlic
1 tablespoon finely chopped fresh parsley
1 tablespoon finely chopped fresh dill
1 tablespoon finely chopped chives
1 tablespoon finely chopped fresh basil
1 tablespoon finely chopped fresh tarragon
freshly ground black pepper, to taste
salt, to taste

Heat the olive oil in a skillet over a high heat until very hot. Add the zucchini slices and cook, stirring frequently, until tender, about 5 minutes. Season with salt and pepper, stir again and remove from the skillet with a slotted spoon. Drain the zucchini in a colander or sieve.

Melt the margarine in the skillet. Return the drained zucchini to the skillet and add the garlic, parsley, chives, dill, basil and tarragon. Toss well, transfer to a serving dish and serve hot. Serves 6.

Sautéed Sweet Potatoes
with Shallots

2 pounds sweet potatoes
7 tablespoons low-fat margarine
8 shallots, quartered
3/4 cup low-salt chicken broth
freshly ground black pepper, to taste

Peel the sweet potatoes and cut them into 1/4-inch slices. Cut each slice into quarters.

Melt 3 tablespoons of the margarine in a skillet over a moderately high heat. Add half the sweet potatoes and sauté until they are light brown, about 8 to 10 minutes. Remove the sweet potatoes from the skillet and put them in a bowl. Add 3 more tablespoons of margarine to the skillet and cook the remaining sweet potatoes as above.

Melt the remaining tablespoon of margarine in the skillet over a moderate heat. Add the shallots and sauté until light brown, about 6 to 8 minutes. Stir in the chicken broth and simmer the mixture, stirring often, until the shallots are cooked and glazed, about 5 minutes.

Raise the heat to moderately high and return the sweet potatoes to the skillet. Cook until they are golden brown and heated through, about 5 minutes. Use a spatula to turn the potatoes. Be sure they heat and brown evenly.

Remove the sweet potato mixture from the skillet and put into a serving dish. Serves 4 to 6.

Roasted Corn with Herbs

3/4 cup softened low-fat margarine
1 1/2 tablespoons finely chopped fresh parsley
1 1/2 tablespoons finely chopped fresh chives
1 1/2 tablespoons finely chopped scallions,
    white parts only
1 1/2 teaspoons fresh lemon juice
1/2 teaspoon Tabasco sauce
Worcestershire sauce, to taste
8 ears fresh corn
freshly ground black pepper, to taste
salt, to taste

Put the margarine, parsley, chives, scallions, lemon juice, salt, Tabasco sauce, Worcestershire sauce and pepper into a bowl. Mix until well-blended. Cover the bowl and refrigerate for 1 to 2 hours.

Prepare coals, the broiler or the gas grill for roasting. Remove the margarine from the refrigerator.

Pull back the corn husks from the ears, but do not detach them. Remove the corn silks from the ears. Spread each ear of corn with 1 tablespoon of the herb margarine. Carefully wrap the husks back around the ears and wrap each ear in aluminum foil.

Roast the corn over hot coals or in a broiler or gas grill 4 inches from the heat source until tender, about 30 minutes. Turn the ears frequently.

When done, remove the aluminum foil. Pull off the husks and brush the corn with additional margarine. Serves 4.

Mushrooms Sautéed in Sherry

2 tablespoons low-fat margarine
2 tablespoons olive oil
3/4 pound fresh mushrooms, thickly sliced
1/2 cup coarsely chopped onions
1 cup dry sherry
1 tablespoon finely chopped fresh parsley
freshly ground black pepper, to taste
salt, to taste

Melt the margarine with 1 tablespoon olive oil in a large skillet over a moderately high heat. Add the mushrooms and sauté, stirring often, until softened, about 2 minutes. Using a slotted spoon, remove the mushrooms from the skillet and set aside. Pour off any liquid.

Lower the heat to moderately low and add the remaining olive oil to the skillet. Add the onions and cook until soft but not brown, about 5 minutes. Add the sherry and stir. Raise the heat to high and bring the mixture to a boil. Continue to boil until reduced by half, about 5 to 6 minutes.

Lower the heat again to moderately low. Add the mushrooms to the skillet and season with salt and pepper. Simmer gently for 5 minutes. Add the parsley and stir.

Transfer the mushrooms to a serving bowl.
Serves 4 to 6.

Beets with Sweet Onion & Thyme

12 small beets
6 tablespoons low-fat margarine
1 large sweet white onion
2 teaspoons dried thyme or 1 tablespoon fresh thyme
1 tablespoon sugar
2 tablespoons white wine vinegar
freshly ground black pepper, to taste
salt, to taste

Wash the beets gently and leave 2 inches of the stem on.
    In a large pot, bring a small amount of water to boil.
Add the beets; the water should not cover all of them.
Cover and reduce the heat. Simmer for 35 to 45 minutes
or until the beets feel tender when touched. As soon as
the beets are done, drain them and cover them with cold
water. When they are cool enough to handle, take the
skins off and cut them into thin slices.
    Transfer the beets to a saucepan. Add the margarine,
onion, thyme, sugar, vinegar and salt and pepper. Heat
until margarine is melted and beets are heated. Adjust
seasonings to taste. Serves 4 to 6.

Leeks Au Gratin

18 small leeks, roots and tough stems trimmed off
1/4 cup softened low-calorie margarine
1/2 cup fine bread crumbs
1/2 cup freshly grated Parmesan cheese
1 tablespoon Dijon mustard
3/4 teaspoon freshly ground black pepper
1/2 teaspoon salt

Cut the white portion of the leeks in half and wash thoroughly.

Bring a saucepan of water to a boil. Add the leeks, reduce the heat and simmer for about 5 minutes or until the leeks are just tender. Drain.

Preheat the oven to 400 degrees F. Lightly grease a shallow casserole using some of the margarine. Spread the leeks in the casserole and season them with salt and pepper. Toss the bread crumbs and Parmesan and sprinkle the mixture evenly over the leeks. Combine the remaining margarine and mustard together until they are mixed well. Dot this mixture over the top of the leeks.

Bake the leeks for 20 minutes or until golden and bubbly. Serves 6.

Baked Eggplant

1 large eggplant
flour for dredging
1/3 to 1/2 cup olive oil
1 large onion, thinly sliced
2 cloves of garlic, finely chopped
4 tablespoons olive oil
2 cups imported canned Italian plum tomatoes, drained
1 orange or yellow sweet pepper, finely chopped
2 tablespoons chopped fresh basil
1/2 cup dried toasted bread crumbs
1/2 cup freshly grated Parmesan cheese
pepper, to taste
salt, to taste

Lightly grease a 2 to 3 quart casserole with olive oil.
Cut the eggplant into 1/2-inch slices. Dredge the slices in flour.
In a large skillet heat 1/3 cup of the olive oil. Place a few slices of the eggplant in the skillet at a time and sauté until nicely browned on each side, this could take 5 minutes per side. Add more olive oil as needed. As the slices are done, remove them to drain and season with salt and pepper to taste.
In a medium skillet sauté the onion and garlic in the remaining 4 tablespoons of olive oil until the onion is wilted.
Preheat the oven to 300 degrees F.
Beginning with the eggplant, arrange layers in the casserole of eggplant, onion, tomatoes and pepper. Season with the chopped basil. Cover the casserole and bake for 1 hour.
Remove the cover and sprinkle with the bread crumbs. Return to the oven for 15 minutes. Remove from the oven again, and sprinkle with Parmesan cheese. Return to the oven for an additional 10 to 15 minutes or until golden. Serves 6.

Roasted Baby Onions & Beets

20 small red beets
25 pearl onions
1/4 cup olive oil
1 teaspoon ground orange peel
1/2 teaspoon coriander
freshly ground black pepper, to taste
salt, to taste

Preheat the oven to 375 degrees F.
Wash and carefully trim the beets. Plunge the pearl onions into a pot of boiling water for 1 minute. Remove from the heat, rinse with cold water and push out of their skins.
Combine the beets and the onions in a rectangular casserole or roasting pan. Pour the olive oil over them and toss until beets and onions are coated.
Add the salt, pepper, orange peel and coriander. Toss again.
Bake uncovered in the oven for 40 to 50 minutes, or until the vegetables are brown and tender. Stir occasionally. Transfer to a serving dish. Serves 6.

New Potato & Escarole Sauté

8 medium-size new potatoes
2 tablespoons low-fat margarine
1 tablespoon chopped garlic in oil
4 cups escarole, washed shredded and tightly packed
freshly ground black pepper, to taste
salt, to taste

Wash and quarter the potatoes. In a large pot of boiling water cook the potatoes until just tender. Remove from the heat, drain and rinse with cold water. When cool enough to handle, cut the quarters into 4 to 6 slices.

In a large skillet, melt the margarine add the garlic, then potatoes. Add salt and pepper to taste. Sauté the potatoes until they are heated, about 2 to 3 minutes. Add the escarole and stir until wilted, about 1 to 2 minutes. Serves 6.

Vegetarian Baked Beans

3 cups dry navy beans
water, to cover
2 teaspoons cider vinegar
2 large white onions, chopped
1 teaspoon dry mustard
3/4 cup dark molasses

Place the beans in a large pot with enough water to cover. Cover the pot and over a high heat bring the mixture to a boil, for 2 to 3 minutes. Remove from the heat and let stand covered for 1 hour.

Preheat the oven to 300 degrees F.

In a large oven-proof casserole combine the beans, 3 cups of cold water, the vinegar, onions, mustard and molasses. Mix well. Cover and allow the beans to bake for 5 hours or until done. Check every hour, add more water as needed. Serves 6 to 8.

Lentils with Thyme & Garlic

1 cup lentils
water, to cover
1 tablespoon minced garlic
2 teaspoons olive oil
1/4 cup fresh lime juice
1 tablespoon fresh thyme
coarsely ground pepper to taste

Place the lentils in a large pot with water to cover. Cover
the pot and bring to a boil, remove the cover and cook
over a moderate heat for 15 to 20 minutes or until done.
The lentils should be firm but tender. Drain and reserve.
   In a large skillet, sauté the garlic in the olive oil for
1 minute. Add the lentils to the skillet and the lime juice,
thyme and pepper. Mix well and let cool. Serves 4.

Lentil Stew with Brown Rice

1 tablespoon olive oil
1 large onion, finely chopped
1 tablespoon minced garlic
1 cup finely chopped carrots
1/2 cup finely chopped celery
2 boneless and skinless chicken breasts, cut into cubes
1 1/2 cups low-fat chicken broth
1 1/2 cups water
1 cup lentils
1/2 cup dry white wine
1 tablespoon fresh thyme
1 cup brown rice
1 teaspoon freshly ground black pepper
salt, if desired

Heat oil in a deep skillet or saucepan, add the onion and garlic, sauté for 2 minutes. Add carrots, celery and chicken cubes, sauté for 5 to 7 minutes or until cubes are evenly brown and vegetables have softened.

Add the chicken broth, water, lentils, and wine to the skillet. Season with pepper, thyme and salt. Add enough water to the skillet to cover all ingredients, bring to a boil. Add the rice, cover and reduce heat. Cook for 40 to 45 minutes or until rice and lentils are tender but firm. Serves 6.

Turkey Loaf

2 teaspoons olive oil
2 cloves garlic, chopped
1/2 cup fresh basil, chopped
2 pounds ground turkey
1/2 cup rolled oats
2 tablespoons Dijon style mustard
1/4 cup white wine
2 egg whites, lightly beaten
coarsely ground pepper, to taste
salt, to taste

Preheat oven to 375 degrees F. Spray a casserole or loaf
pan with low-calorie cooking spray. Set aside.

In a small skillet heat the oil, add the garlic and sauté
for 2 to 3 minutes. Remove from the heat and transfer to a
large bowl.

To the garlic add the basil, turkey, oats, mustard,
wine, egg whites, salt and pepper. Mix very well. If
mixture is too tight add some additional wine or water.
Place in prepared pan and smooth into shape.

Bake for 1 hour or until golden. Serves 6.

Black Bean Chili

1 1/2 pounds lean ground beef
1 onion, chopped
1 clove garlic, chopped
1 cup imported Italian tomatoes, drained
    and coarsely chopped
1/4 cup tomato sauce
2 tablespoons chili powder
2 cups black beans, canned or cooked, well drained
freshly ground black pepper, to taste
salt, to taste

In a large non-stick skillet, sauté the meat until brown, then remove from the skillet with a slotted spoon to a bowl and reserve. To the same skillet add the onion and garlic, sauté for 5 minutes or until both have softened. Using a spatula to hold the onion and garlic in place, carefully drain off any remaining fat. Return the meat to the skillet.

Add the tomatoes, tomato sauce, chili powder, salt and pepper. Mix well.

Bring the mixture to a boil, reduce heat , cover and simmer for 30 minutes.

Add the beans and adjust the seasoning. Cook for an additional 5 minutes, uncovered. Serves 6.

Cocido

2 tablespoons olive oil
3 to 4 pounds chicken parts, cleaned, skinned, all visible
fat removed
1 pound seasoned turkey sausage, cut into bite-size pieces
1 onion, finely chopped
2 cloves garlic, chopped
1 small head green cabbage, coarsely chopped
2 carrots, cut in 2-inch pieces
1/2 cup white wine
1/2 cup water
2 cups chick peas, canned or cooked, well drained
freshly ground black pepper, to taste
salt, to taste

In a large skillet heat the olive oil. Add the chicken pieces
and sauté until golden on all sides, about 5 to 7 minutes.
Transfer to a large stew or stock pot.

Add the turkey sausage to the skillet, sauté for 3 to 5
minutes or until golden. Transfer to pot with the chicken.

Add the onion and garlic to the skillet, sauté for
5 minutes or until soft and golden, transfer to pot.

Add chopped cabbage to pot, stir well. Add the carrots. Pour in the wine and water, season with salt and
pepper, mix well. Bring the mixture to a boil, reduce heat,
cover and simmer for 55 minutes, stir occasionally.

Add the chick peas and adjust the seasoning. Cook
uncovered for 5 minutes longer or until chicken is done.
Serves 6 to 8.

Bulghur with Spinach, Mushrooms & Onions

1 cup bulghur, rinsed with cold water, drain
2 cups cold water
2 tablespoons olive oil
1 onion, sliced
1 pound leaf spinach, cleaned and stemmed
1 cup sliced button mushrooms
2 teaspoons sesame oil
black pepper, to taste
salt, to taste

In a medium saucepan combine the water and bulghur, bring to a boil, cover and simmer for 40 minutes or until all the water has been absorbed. Remove from the heat, uncover and place 2 sheets of paper towel across the top of the pot. Cover and set aside.

In a large skillet heat the olive oil, add the onion and sauté for 5 minutes or until soft. Add the spinach and sauté for 3 minutes or until wilted. Add the mushrooms and cook an additional 3 to 5 minutes or until soft.

Add the bulghur to the skillet stir well and separate the grains. Season with salt, pepper and sesame oil. Cook for an additional 2 to 3 minutes or until bulghur is heated. Serves 4 to 6.

Couscous

4 tablespoons olive oil
1 4-pound chicken, cut into serving pieces, skinned,
  all visible fat removed
2 large onions, chopped
3 cloves garlic, minced
1 large can Italian plum tomatoes, with liquid
1 cup carrots, sliced
1 teaspoon freshly grated nutmeg
2 cups chickpeas, canned or cooked, well drained
1 cup quick-cooking couscous
pepper, to taste
salt, to taste

In a large stew or stock pot, heat the oil. Add chicken
pieces and cook for 5 minutes or until brown on all sides.
Add the onion, garlic, tomatoes with liquid and carrots.
Season with salt, pepper and nutmeg, mix well. Cover and
simmer for 1 hour or until chicken is very tender. When
the chicken has approximately 5 to 10 minutes of cooking
time left, stir in the chickpeas.

While the chicken is cooking prepare the couscous
according to package directions. Arrange the stew on a
bed of couscous. Serves 4 to 6.

Barley Casserole

4 tablespoons low-fat margarine
1 cup button mushrooms, sliced
1 large white onion, chopped
1 red bell pepper, cored and chopped
1 1/2 cups pearl barley
3 1/2 cups low-fat chicken broth
2 tablespoons minced parsley
pepper, to taste
salt, to taste

In a large non-stick saucepan heat the margarine over a medium heat, add mushrooms and sauté for 3 minutes. Add the onions and red pepper and cook until soft, about 5 minutes.

Add the barley and cook over a medium heat until the barley is lightly browned. Add the chicken broth, cover and simmer for 50 minutes to 1 hour or until all the liquid has been absorbed and the barley is tender. Add salt, pepper and parsley. Serves 6.

Spiced Scallops
with Curly Endive

1 clove garlic, chopped
1 large onion, peeled and finely chopped
1 sweet red pepper, peeled, seeded and julienned
2 tablespoons olive oil
1 pound sea scallops, halved if large
1 teaspoon Tabasco sauce
1 1/2 pounds curly endive, washed and coarsely shredded
2 tablespoons olive oil
freshly ground black pepper, to taste

In a large sauté pan, gently fry the garlic, onions and red
pepper in the olive oil until soft, but not brown. Set aside.
In the same pan, sauté the scallops over medium high
heat until seared and just cooked through, about 4 to 5
minutes. Return the vegetable mixture to the pan and
cover, off the heat.

Add the other 2 tablespoons of olive oil. Sauté the
curly endive until limp and hot through. Arrange on a
platter and top with the scallop-vegetable mixture. Season
liberally with freshly ground black pepper. Serves 4.

Whole Wheat Pasta Primavera

There are a thousand-and-one recipes for pasta primavera (springtime pasta). The choice of vegetables depends entirely on what's available, but all should be young and in prime condition.

2 tablespoons olive oil
2 cloves garlic, peeled and chopped
1 small onion, thinly sliced
1 cup mushrooms, thinly sliced
1 small zucchini, julienned
1 small carrot, julienned
1 cup broccoli flowerets
2 tomatoes, peeled, seeded and chopped
1 cup string beans, sliced lengthwise
1 cup asparagus tips
1 1/2 pounds whole wheat spaghetti or penne
salt and pepper, to taste

In a very large skillet, heat the olive oil .
    Sauté the garlic, onions and mushrooms until soft and golden. Add all the other vegetables and toss over high heat until just crisp and hot. Pour over the pasta and season with salt and pepper. Serve immediately.
    If you wish to make a salad to be served at room temperature, toss pasta with vegetables, add another 1/2 cup of olive oil and vinegar to taste and let marinate for an hour before serving. Serves 6.

Spiced Stuffed Figs in Port

1/2 cup chopped nuts (almonds or pecans are best)
3 tablespoons low-fat margarine
2 tablespoons brown sugar
1 pound dried figs
1 cup ruby port

In a bowl, cream together the nuts, margarine and brown sugar.

Make a small incision in each fig and stuff with a teaspoonful of the nut mixture.

Place the figs in a baking dish and pour over the port. Cover the dish with foil and bake in a 350 degree F. oven for about 20 minutes. Let cool.

Arrange the figs on individual serving plates and pour some of the port over each. Serves 6.